Change Management f
The No Waffle Guide To Managing
By Louise Pal

CW00968072

Table of Contents

Types of Change

There are two different types of change, planned and emergent. In the 1940's Kurt Lewin developed the notion of planned change. He suggested that change is deliberately planned and subsequently embarked upon in organisations (Marrow 1977). They can move from one stable state to another in a pre-planned manner.

Emergent change does not see change as a planned event, instead it views change as a continuous process. This a more realistic view of how many workplaces experience change in today's climate. If you can encourage your employees to view change as the norm, they will be far more receptive to changes you introduce in the workplace.

Five Laws of Organisation Development

There are five laws of organisation development in relation to workplace change or transition:

1. An individual may cope well with the changes initially but this could change at any moment. At the beginning of the change programme, the individual might have appeared to be coping well with the changes, however, as time progresses the continued uncertainty is straining their personal resources.

2. Successful outcomes will no doubt encourage challenge. Success leads to change. Change can be challenging whether it is considered positive or negative. The organisation might not have the resources to manage the changes. This is often seen when a company undergoes rapid growth.

3. The underlying factors that resulted in its success may now be causing its demise. Organisations often outgrow their current processes forcing changes to occur.

4. Usually troubled times = developmental change. When an organisation is experiencing troubled times, it is usually because there is a need for change in order to adapt to the new situation. Alternatively, a change process might already be taking place.

5. Not recognising or engaging with the need for change. Organisations need to future proof their product or services. Not moving with the times can leave the competition with a clear advantage.

Transition Management Process – Involving the Employees

It is important that organisations ensure people are involved in the transition management process as it helps to support the new beginning by:

1. Ensuring the employee understands the underlying reasons why the organization has to embark on the planned changes. This insight can gain the employees support as they realise it is in the best interests of the company.

2. The employees will more likely want to join forces with the management to make the changes a success, rather than fighting against them.

3. The employees will be more willing to share their knowledge and insights on how to improve products or services. In addition they might have ideas as to how to improve efficiency and cut costs on the front line.

4. By discussing the changes with the employees, the organisation is better placed to incorporate the employees' desires and needs in to the change. This is likely to result in higher levels of morale.

5. Everyone who plays a part is responsible for the outcome.

Resistance to Change

Consider the concept 'people resist change'. Do you resist change? In answering this question, it can help to recall times in your life when you have experienced change. If you did resist change, what was it about the changes that you resisted? Were there changes that you did not resist? What was it about these changes that made you not resist them?

Reviewing your notes consider whether you agree with the statement 'people resist change.'

Do People Resist Change?

People do not always resist change. It is a mental model that has become ingrained (Dent & Goldberg 1999). A mental model is a collection of thoughts as to how something operates in the world. People are often unaware that they use these mental models and presume that they are in fact reality. Although it is widely believed that people will always resist change, there is actually very little evidence to suggest this is the case.

It could be that the concept of resistance to change has been passed down, as Kuhn (1970) suggests. Dent & Galloway's (1999) support this suggestion. They conducted an analysis of management textbooks. They discovered that the term 'resistance to change' was in the vast majority of textbooks as a given fact, rather than as a concept that needed exploring. In general, people very rarely resist change which results in positive outcomes in their lives. They are far more likely to resist change which will affect their lives in a negative manner. People don't resist change, they resist loses.

Coch and French (1948) conducted a study in a pyjama factory in Virginia. They wanted to investigate why people resist change and how this resistance could be managed. The title of this piece of work was 'Overcoming Resistance to Change' and this is where the term originated from. Their research concluded that when employees were involved in the process, they were less likely to resist the changes.

The study increased the popularity of the concept of 'resistance to change'. It is claimed that the researchers were simply illustrating that it was beneficial to involve employees in the change process. They were not inferring that employees will consistently resist change.

ADKAR

When an organisation is going through a change process, the employees may well support the notion of the new changes and wish to work hard to make the changes successful. However, various obstacles can prevent successful change from occurring.

ADKAR was developed by Prosci in 1998. ADKAR is a tool which enables organisations to analyse how employees are managing the changes and if there are particular aspects they are finding problematic. Once the aspect has been identified, work can begin to overcome the obstacles that the employee is facing. The elements are:

Awareness
Desire
Knowledge
Ability
Reinforcement

Consider an employee who is affected by the change programme. It might be useful to consider a particular individual if you suspect they currently have, or might have in the future, difficulties with change.

Note down your responses to the following:

Awareness of the need to change: To what degree is the individual aware of the reasons for the organisational change (1 - 5 where 1 is no awareness and 5 is total awareness).

Desire to make the change happen: From the individual's perspective, list the possible outcomes that they might be predicting as a result of the change. Consider both the positive and negative outcomes. Analyse the list as a whole and rate his/her desire to change on a 1 - 5 scale.

Knowledge about how to change: Consider to what extent the person truly understands how their working life will differ as a result of the organisational changes. Contemplate the skills and knowledge the individual will require in order for them to adapt to the changes successfully. Rate this person's knowledge or level of training in these areas on a 1 to 5 scale.

Ability to change: Consider if the individual has the ability to utilise the skills and knowledge they hold in order to adapt to the changes successfully. Rate this person's ability to implement the new skills, knowledge and behaviours to support the change on a 1 - 5 scale.

Ability to change: Consider if the individual is able to successfully manage the changes required by drawing on their own resources, skills and knowledge. Rate on a 1 to 5 scale, the extent to which other activities are reinforcing and supporting the change.

Can identify which aspects of the change the individual requires further assistance with? This might be further training or changes in organisational processes to align fully to the change process. An action plan can then be devised.

You might find it useful to use the ADKAR process to analyse three or more other team members. You can then compare your results and assess whether the ADKARs are similar. If some aspects of the ADKAR are similar, it will highlight if there are any particular elements of the change programme that require further evaluation. It can also indicate how your team members are coping differently with the changes taking place in the organisation.

Emotions to Expect During Change Programmes

Recall a time when you have experienced changes within the workplace. Even if there is not a large scale change programme that you have as a reference, many organisations experience various elements of change.

What emotions did you or team experience? What emotions are employees likely to experience during change programmes? For each emotion that you have listed, try to speculate as to why this emotion would occur.

GRASS

Grass illustrates some common emotions that are experienced during a period of change:

Guilt
Resentment
Anxiety
Self Absorption
Stress

Guilt

Managers often experience feelings of guilt as they have had to make people redundant, transfer them to different departments or reduce their responsibilities. Employees can experience guilt too if they have remained in their position yet their colleagues have lost their jobs.

When experiencing feelings of guilt, managers might make an extra effort to display acts of kindness. They might refrain from providing negative feedback even though it is required. Alternatively, some managers may opt to suppress feelings of guilt which could result in an increase of aggressive behaviours.

Resentment

Resentment can build during a change process. Both managers and managed can feel resentment at the upheaval the change has imposed. This is a natural reaction to the losses the individuals are experiencing. These negative emotions can build up and soak into the very core of the organisation if it is not managed sensitively.

Anxiety

Anxiety is another natural reaction as people fear what the future will bring and long for the stability of the past. Feelings of anxiety can result in lower levels of motivation, concentration, performance and creativity. It can also result in higher than usual error and accident rates.

Self-absorption

Self-absorption – If people are feeling nervous about the changes, they are more likely to focus inwards, resulting in self-absorption. They lose interest and concern for others which in a work environment can affect team work, customer service and product/service quality.

Stress

Stress is a common emotion experienced during the change process. High levels of stress can result in similar outcomes of both anxiety and self-absorption. It has a high risk of resulting in ill health due to the many diseases that are caused or aggravated by stress.

Stages of Response (Kubler Ross 1973)

There are different stages of response when people experience change. Kubler Ross studied people who were suffering with fatal cancer. She discovered that on hearing the news people would initially be in denial. This was followed by anger, then bargaining, depression and finally acceptance.

Research has shown that people experiencing any type of change, pass through similar stages. As change can often result in experiencing a loss of some kind, they are prone to feelings of grief. In Kubler's research the loss was the loss of life. In relation to the workplace, this loss might relate to reduced working hours or threat of redundancy. The stages that people pass through in an organisational change context are: shock, defensive retreat, acknowledgement and finally adaption and change.

1. Shock

The first reaction is one of shock as they realise their current situation, in which they feel secure, is under threat. This stage tends to evoke feelings of anxiety as they solely focus on potential loses and how this might impact of their lives. This anxiety impacts on their performance, productivity and general well being.

2. Defensive Retreat

In an attempt to stop the change from happening, people attempt to hold on to the old processes and procedures.

3. Acknowledgement

At this stage people start to let go and begin to investigate how they can manage the changes imposed upon them.

4. Adaption & Change

Finally people have adapted to the new situation, together with its new processes and procedures.

The Three Phase Process of Change

Bridges (1991, 2003) suggests there are 3 phases people pass through during organisational change. These three phrases are:

1. Letting Go
2. Neutral Zone - This is the in-between time.
3. New Beginning

Letting Go

In the current situation, before the change, the individual feels secure. They are confident and comfortable as they have all the knowledge and skills to complete the job successfully. Any future plans for progression or personal development are based on the current state.

It is vitally important at this stage to identify and prepare for the losses the individual will experience as a result of the change. Failure to do so can greatly hinder the success of an organisational change programme.

Identifying losses

Sometimes these losses are not obvious at first glance. Managers need to be careful not to put their own judgements on to the losses of others and deem them unimportant. It is important that managers are very clear about what will and will not change. This clears up any confusion and reduces the risk of rumours spreading. It is important to acknowledge the losses that individuals will experience and show empathy.

Write a list of what your team members might lose as a result of the planned changes.

What are individuals losing? Is everyone losing the same things or are people losing different things? What is the team losing?

Acknowledge the Past

Speak of the past in a positive light. Keep in mind that many people will think fondly of the past and will fiercely defend it if it is attacked. This defense will further increase resistance to change.

Ensure that people do not have to let go of everything old. It might mean a bit of creativity is needed in order to allow something old to remain.

Acknowledge how the previous way of working brought success to the business. Reconfirm the reasons behind the need for the change and emphasise any similarities between the past, present and future.

Acknowledge emotions

- Ensure you fully listen to people's perspectives on what they are losing. Don't dismiss their perspective. Disagreeing with the way they see things will create tension and is unlikely to change their mind at this stage

Expect over reactions, expect anger.

Expect anxiety. Consider if some individuals might be concerned that they are not capable of carrying out the tasks that will be required. Is there the possibility that training, mentoring or coaching could bridge any skills gaps?

Change cause losses. It is these losses that the people are reacting to, not the changes. Ignoring the existence of such losses can cause problems.

Try to achieve the following actions

Provide information in a variety of formats such as letters, memos, newsletters, intranet, meetings and presentations. Do not presume that because the employees were informed by one letter that every individual has memorised all the key points. It is important to reinforce the message.

Remember to reiterate the reasons the organization is making these changes. If possible let them experience it first-hand. For example, if the change is as a result of customer complaints, show them the customer complaint data. Ensure they appreciate the changes are urgent.

Consider if there is anything that could be given to compensate for the losses experienced. This could be status, recognition, mentoring, training etc.

The initial changes that take place might cause secondary changes. These can be less obvious to the managers, yet matter a great deal to the individuals. If an employee appears to be resisting the changes, it may be that a secondary change is the cause.

As an example of a secondary change consider an individual who currently enjoys long lunch breaks. They presently work in a room separate to their manager so nobody takes note of when they leave or return from lunch. They have been using this to their full advantage and have been taking at least 1 ½ hours for lunch every day. The changes will require them to move into the office with their manager. This in turn will require them to take lunch in the allotted time. This individual might be creating a lot of resistance about moving office, yet the management can't understand why. In this situation the management would continue as planned and the individual will eventually adapt to the new way of working. Other secondary changes can be changed to make the individual more comfortable with the changes.

Consider what secondary changes could exist within your work place. Make an exhaustive list.

Neutral Zone

Next is the neutral zone. This is the in-between phase, where the old methods of working are no longer appropriate and the new methods are not fully functional.

Kotter (1995) studied over 100 organisations experiencing organisational change. Kotter reported that often employees supported the changes and wished to help the organisation make the changes a success, however they were facing various obstacles which were impacting on their ability to make the required changes.

Various aspects of the role might not be aligned with the new vision. In order to understand any obstacles that the employees are facing, managers can ask what is helping and what is hindering the change efforts. In doing so, other departments can learn from their experiences and obstacles can be managed more effectively. By doing so employees are more likely to feel committed to the change goals, feel part of a team and take responsibility for the changes required (Carnall 1990).

 Managers should enquire about obstacles regularly. As the individual moves through the change process they can discover obstacles that were not apparent at the beginning.

There is a great deal of psychological change during the neutral zone as viewpoints are altered and the past starts to give way to the future.

What problems do you envisage employees experiencing in the neutral zone? What emotions might employees experience? What impact could this have on the work?

Dangers of the Neutral Zone

There are many dangers of the neutral zone:

- High anxiety levels
- Low motivation
- Emotions run high – employees often over-analyse or make negative predictions
- Sick days increase as employees struggle to manage this unsettling period
- Weaknesses previously hidden are suddenly exposed

On a positive note, it is also a very creative time. At times employees and managers can get stuck in old patterns of working that are largely ineffective. One great benefit of the neutral zone is the freedom to improve processes and procedures.

Leading People through the Neutral Zone

When thinking about change people usually expect to move from the old to the new instantly. They fail to realise that there will be a period of uncertainty in between. One of the manager's roles during a change programme is to educate their team members that a neutral zone exists. This awareness will help their employees accept the uncertainty during this period.

Discussions regarding the neutral zone may include how to manage obstacles that have not been foreseen. It can also be useful to discuss expected emotions during this period. Plans can be developed in order to manage this often confusing period. These plans could include temporary systems.

If employees have a clear vision of how the period of the neutral zone is enabling them to move towards the overall change goals, they are more likely to manage the change effectively. employees are unable to see how a change contributes to the achievement of the overall vision, it can cause distress. Unexpected changes can also unsettle them.

The neutral zone is a period of turbulence. Whilst some people can enjoy the freedom of this period, others will find it deeply unsettling. It can be very tempting to rush through it as quickly as possible in order to regain stability. This might involve pushing for quick decisions rather than spending time investigating the best solutions for the organisation.

Throughout the neutral zone it is important that managers clearly communicate with their team. It helps to reduce risk and ambiguity (Pugh 1993). A lack of communication can result in people trying to mind-read managers or predict the future. This can result in negative rumours spreading through the organisation raising anxiety levels even further. The repeated use of memo's, meetings, newsletters and presentations can help to clearly communicate and reinforce the plans.

Goals from personal appraisals or reward schemes will need to be reviewed in order to ensure they align to the neutral zone. Previous goals, rewards, policies, procedures and even roles may reinforce the old methods. Temporary goals and systems are sometimes required to enable a smooth transition through the neutral zone, before being changed again for the New Beginning.

The setting of short term goals can be used to guide people through the neutral zone and create a sense of achievement. This can provide an additional motivating benefit as the employees can see the changes are starting to work.

Managing Conflict In the Neutral Zone

During the neutral zone, the heightened negative emotions can result in more conflicts occurring. This might relate to people feeling insecure, anxious or under threat. They might also still be grieving about the losses they have incurred. When in a conflict situation allow the individual to inform you of their concerns, do not interrupt. This information can be a great insight into how others are also feeling, yet are reluctant to share with you. Listen intently and assess whether you can fix any of the points raised. Showing this commitment to listening and actively trying to improve things for the individual, will help to keep communication channels open in the future.

New Beginning

The New Beginning stage marks the fact that the changes are operational and new working practices have been incorporated into the workplace. People discover the new way of working and experience the new energy it creates. This can be an exciting time yet it is not without its dangers. Certain anxieties can reside around the new beginning. People may remember the past, when they tried something new and failed. If this is the case managers can remind them of the problems that existed and why the change was needed in the first place. They can create a vision of the future and reinforce the benefits these changes will bring. Providing support and adequate training, to ensure employees have the capability to carry out the new tasks required of them, is essential.

Individuals might be concerned that the future state does not match their personal development plans. For example, an employee may have been undertaking formal training which now appears less relevant to their new role or they may realise that their chances of promotion have decreased due to fewer higher level roles. If this is the case consider what you can replace this 'loss' with. Perhaps you can offer coaching and mentoring to further their development, might there be alternative promotion opportunities in the future, would the person like to take on more managerial responsibilities to gain skills and experience,is there a training course they would like to pursue, etc?

Why Transformation Efforts Fail

Studies have been conducted on organisational change for decades. Kotter (1995) has identified 8 common errors that decrease the effectiveness and success of change programmes.

Error 1: Failure to create a sense of urgency.

If employees feel that there is no urgency to the change, a feeling of malaise can occur which can de-motivate and slow down the change process. This in turn can lead to an overall unsuccessful outcome. Urgency can be created through the use of customer data, financial data and reviews of the competition.

Error 2: Not creating a powerful enough group of guiding leaders.

You need to have an influential group of people to manage the change process. Usually it is best to involve line managers as they have influence within their own teams and can provide insight into how the separate sections of the organisation operate as a whole. The group can be fairly small for example 3-5 people, or considerably larger for large organisations.

Error 3: Lacking a vision.

The change management team need to create a simple vision for the future. If it is too complicated people will not be able to comprehend its many parts and will tend to simplify the version in their own minds. This can lead to misunderstandings and confusion when the change programme is undertaken. Ideally you will be able to communicate the **overall** vision and the subsequent plans in under 5 minutes.

Additional time will be required when explaining the finer details relevant to each department.

Error 4: Under-communicating the vision by a factor of ten.

On some occasions change plans are communicated in one single meeting. This is not enough for employees to fully digest the vision and subsequent plans. It needs to be reinforced continually. This can be achieved by managers acting as role models and continually demonstrating the new working practices.

Error 5: Not removing obstacles to the new vision.

Sometimes obstacles can make people choose between working towards the new vision or serving their own self-interest. This can occur if a reward system does not get realigned to the new way of working. The employee then faces the dilemma of working the new way and not receiving rewards, or working the old way and receiving their rewards.

Managers might not be fully engaged in the new initiatives and instead just pay them lip service. This can keep the old methods of working alive, damaging the likelihood of successful outcomes from the change efforts.

Error 6: Not systematically creating short term wins.

Create short term goals so people can experience short term wins. Sometimes change programmes can take years from start to finish. If people do not experience a sense of achievement and a feeling of progression, momentum can falter. Ensuring they experience short term wins can keep them motivated and encourage them to maintain a sense of urgency.

Error 7: Declaring victory too soon.

Initial results could indicate that it appears that the change has been successful but it is important that these initial results are not blown out of proportion. Whilst managers should celebrate this achievement, the need for continuing the change needs to be communicated. It can take 5 to 10 years before the changes soak into the core of the organisation. If success is declared too early, the change efforts can start to fade. Traditional ways of working seep back in and the organisation starts to slip back to the previous state.

Error 8: Not anchoring changes in the organisations culture.

It is vital that managers continually reinforce the changes by acting as a role model and encouraging their team members to work with the new practices. It is important they regularly remind employees of the current and future impact of the changes.

Appreciative Inquiry Method for Change Programmes

Activity
Consider that your organisation wishes to embark upon a change programme. The aim of the change programme might be to increase efficiency or profits. For the purpose of this activity, choose one primary aim.

Consider the process of how you would design the change process. Think about:

Who would be involved?
How would the aims, objectives and goals be decided upon?
Would it look to 'fix' problems within company? If so, how would you know what to fix?
Would input from the employees inform the change programme? Keep these answers in mind as you will be asked to refer to them later on.

What is Appreciative Inquiry?

Appreciative Inquiry (A.I.) was developed by Cooperrider and Srivastva (1987). A.I. is a positive focused method used in change programmes. It is considered to be both a philosophy and a methodology. Many companies are now using Appreciative Inquiry to release the potential in their business and the potential in their employees. A.I. can be used on large scale change programmes across organisations or smaller group based projects. A.I. is often more effective than traditional change efforts.

Appreciative Inquiry uses a strength based approach. It is different to traditional problem solving approaches. Appreciative Inquiry reflects on what people value. It creates an organisation around what the members want it to be. It is based on the notion that an organisation will develop in the direction of what it focuses upon. This focus infiltrates how the questions are phrased to itself and its employees (Cooperrider 1990).

The method works on the premise that it is just as important to reflect on the future, as it is to reflect on the past. Reflecting on the future is termed 'Anticipatory Reality'. When individuals are able to speak about what really matters to them, real change is more likely to occur.

Employee Engagement

The Appreciative Inquiry method aims to involve all relevant employees, even if this means involving the whole organisation or group. Every individual is involved from the very beginning. The employees are involved in the whole process from defining to designing to implementing the change. They are therefore also responsible for the outcome and will naturally show higher levels of commitment.

As everybody is involved in the Appreciative Inquiry process, information is disseminated to each and every individual. There is a shared understanding of how the end vision was created. This helps to create open channels of communication throughout the organisation.

A.I. provides individuals with the ability to understand how they fit into the overall strategy. Whilst everyone is working towards their own personal goals, they can see how their personal goals fit into their team and their organisations' overall success. If you compare this to a traditional change programme sometimes this can be difficult and a feeling of separation can occur.

AI encourages the employees of an organisation to work together as a whole in order to achieve the overall aims. This naturally creates a positive work environment which leads to increased performance, productivity, creativity and morale.

The Positive Principle

Organisations need to encourage employees to focus on their positive core. This includes an appraisal of their strengths, successes and visions for the future. Discussions around the ideal future can be a great catalyst for organisational change (Ludema 2001).

If problems are used to drive a change effort, the organisation can find itself with an over whelming number of problems to solve. If a positive focus is used to drive a change effort and creativity is encouraged, this can lead to far greater successful outcomes. Words create worlds (Whitney 1998).

The goal is to build upon the organisations' positive core and incorporate this in to creating a desired vision and plan for the future. This positive approach builds motivation and a desire for change. As a result, appreciative inquiry change efforts often lead to measurable, sustainable results.

Look back over your notes for the Activity earlier in this section. Is it a deficit based approach? Does it look at aspects of the company that are not working and how these could be improved?

If so, spend time considering why the approach you chose is problem focused. Is it the most natural way to initiate change? Is it the way that you engage with change on a personal level? Is it how your organisation currently tries to evoke change? Does change only occur when there are problems to be fixed?

Many people find that when they are looking to make changes they naturally use a problem focused approach. They look at what is wrong and what is not working. Their plans are around how to fix the problem.

Appreciative Inquiry looks at what is working within an organisation and builds upon this. This helps to encourage positive change. It does not focus on problems. What are your initial thoughts on this?

Appreciative Inquiry Critics

When people first hear about Appreciative Inquiry, one of the first criticisms is that 'Sometimes problems have to be fixed. Ignoring them and focusing on the positive isn't going to fix them'.

Appreciative Inquiry can be used to solve identified problems For example, let's say a company's profits are generally down. The solution is to look at how to improve profits. Appreciative Inquiry would look at what parts of the business are most profitable, what is working well in these areas and whether it is possible to apply this to other areas or business products.

Another comment we often hear is, 'If something is NOT working in the organisation then surely we need to identify this? It could be that we focus on solutions and the positive core, but this one thing stops the organisation from moving forward?'

It might be that by focusing on what is working well naturally eradicates what is not working so well. Alternatively if it makes you more comfortable you can first look at problems then re-frame these positively into points of action.

5D Appreciative Inquiry Model

Here is the 5D Appreciative Inquiry Model:

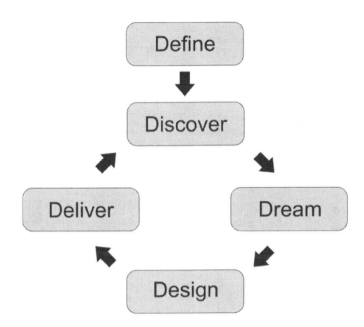

Define

The Define stage looks at identifying aspects to be changed. These aspects might be problems that exist within the organisation or growth opportunities that need exploring.

If the aspect is problem based such as 'poor customer satisfaction', re-frame this to a positive goal such as, 'improving customer satisfaction levels'. Re-framing problems this way is more likely to motivate and encourage commitment from employees.

Discover Phase

The discover phase focuses on:

- Identifying strengths and successes.
- Exploring the highpoints of success.

In the discover phase we collect stories from employees of when the organisation was performing at its most excellent (Bushe 1999):

Let's imagine that a company wishes to improve customer loyalty. The Appreciative Inquiry process would ask employees to share their stories of when customers have remained loyal. This might be individual incidents or it might relate to a period in the past. If the organisation was looking to improve performance levels, stories would be collected relating to when performance levels were high.

This phase also looks at:

- Creating a vision of what success looks like
- Identifying which aspects are of the most personal or material value

Dream Phase

Next is the dream phase. This phase involves:

- Envisioning what could happen.
- Envisioning outcomes.
- Envisioning impacts of these outcomes.

This phase incorporates the elements of the define and discovery phases to develop a shared vision of the dream future. The dream future will ideally detail as much as possible to ensure that people can envisage it fully. The detail also ensures that all those involved in the process are envisioning the same future.

Design Phase

The outputs from the previous define, discover and dream phase are used to inform the design phase. This phase works to plan how the future vision can be achieved. The planning can involve designing roles, structures, initiatives, reward schemes, procedures, processes, policies and mission statements.

Deliver Phase

The deliver phase involves putting the plans from the design phase into action. Change is encouraged, taking care to maintain the positive core. Employees might face challenges in this phase of the process as they adapt to the new working methods.

Appreciative Inquiry in Practice

Ideally the Appreciative Inquiry process would involve the whole organisation Some organisations will take a complete week to complete the define, discover and design stages. This is then followed up with sessions in the weeks and months that follow. Some organisations hire consultants to carry out the process whilst others opt for doing it themselves.

We are now going to look at how to carry out the actual process.

Define Phase

Define your aims for the organisation.

Depending on the situation, you may wish to define your aims with the senior management team and involve the whole organisation at the later discovery phase.

Your objectives might look something like this.........

Your Logo

Objectives - Appreciative Inquiry Session on Date Here

1. To achieve higher customer satisfaction scores.
2. To provide the best service delivery possible.
3. To reinforce our company ethos.
4.
5.
6.

Discover Phase

In the discover phase it is easier to initially work in small groups and then feed back to the larger group.

In addition to this, it is often best for people to take some time to think through their own thoughts before they share them with their small group. This helps the individuals to collect their thoughts with ease. It also helps to ensure that everyone's thoughts are heard.

Below is an example of a handout you could design for the Discover Phase.

Your Logo

Appreciative Inquiry
Discovery Phase

Talk with your group to discover when our organisation was functioning at its best. When telling these stories use as much detail as possible. This will help us to discover the 'positive core' of our organisation.

1. Think of a high point in your working life at this company

_____

_____

_____

2. In that experience what helped you to succeed in relation to:

a) Your strengths

_____

_____

b) The role and nature of the work

_____

_____

c) The organisation

_____

_____

3. What gives 'life' to our organisation. What positive values and beliefs should we build on?

_____

_____

Other questions you might ask in the Discover Phase:

What works well?

What has worked well in the past?

Even if something is not working at the moment, are there aspects of it that are working?

After an Appreciative Inquiry meeting, it can be beneficial to collate the information from the discovery phase and present it to the employees. It could be presented as a document or as a wall display within the workplace. This is used to celebrate and remind all the employees of the strengths of the employees and the company.

Dream Phase

Once the discovery phase has been shared with everyone, it is time to think about the dream phase. This phase involves creating a detailed vision of what an ideal future would look like for the organisation. This is best done in small groups and then fed back to the larger group to collate a 'shared' dream.

Below is an example of a handout you might create for the Dream Phase.

<u>Appreciative Inquiry</u>
<u>Dream Phase</u>

Discuss in your small groups your dreams for the organisation. Refer back to the objectives. You might like to consider:

- What would be an ideal future for the organisation?
- What are the possibilities?
- What would the successful outcomes look like? What would be happening?
- What impact would these successful outcomes have?

Design Phase

Next is the Design Phase. Ideally the large group needs to work together on designing a practical and achievable plan to achieve the dream. You might want to consider:

- Roles
- Structures
- Policies, procedures, processes

- Initiatives
- Training, coaching, mentoring
- Timescales

Deliver Phase

This is the actual doing part. It involves putting into place the action plan that was built around the positive core. Regular meetings and reviews would be beneficial in order to check progress and continue to move things forward.

Future Progressions

As time progresses it might be appropriate to re-visit the discover phase and start the cycle again.

On your own, complete a mini mock run through of the appreciative inquiry process. This activity will act as a revision of the concepts, so do look back through the book in order to inform your plan. Your Appreciative Inquiry Plan would include:

- A list of possible organisation objectives.
- A list of possible questions you would use in the discover and dream phase.
- A mock completion of these questions from your personal perspective.
- A list of the areas you would then need to consider in the design process.
- A mock action plan which includes time scales for action points and follow up meetings.

References

Bridges, W. (1991) Managing Transitions.

Bridges, W. (2003) Making the Most of Change.

Bushe, G. (1999). Five theories of change embedded in appreciative inquiry. In Appreciative Inquiry: Rethinking human organization toward a positive theory of change.

Carnall, C.A, (1990) Managing Change in Organizations, London: Prentice Hall.

Coch,L., French, J.R.P., Jr (1948) Overcoming Resistance to Change. Human Relations, I (4), 512-532.

Cooperrider, D.L (1990). Positive Image, Positive Action: The Affirmative Basis of Organising.

Cooperrider, D. L., & Srivastva, S. (1998). An Invitation to Organizational Wisdom and Executive Courage. In S. Srivastva & D. L. Cooperrider (Eds.).

Dawson, P. (1994) Organisational Change: A Processual Approach. London: Paul Chapman Publishing.

Dent, E.B., Goldberg, S.G. (1999). Challenging "Resistance to Change". Journal of Applied Behavioural Science, 35;21.

Kotter,J.P. (1995) Leading Change. Why Transformation Efforts Fail.

Kübler-Ross, E. (1973) On Death and Dying, Routledge.

Kuhn,T.S. (1970) The Structure of Scientific Revolutions (2nd ed). Chicago: University of Chicago Press.

Ludema, J.(2001). From Deficit Discourse to Vocabularies of Hope: The Power of Appreciation. Appreciative Inquiry: An Emerging Direction for Organisation Development (first ed).

Marrow, A.J. (1977) The Practical Theorist: The Life and Work of Kurt Lewin. New York: Teachers College Press.

Nonaka, I. (1988) Creating Organizational Order out of Chaos: Self Renewal in Japenese Firms' Harvard Business Review, November/December, pp. 96-104.

Pugh, D. (1993) Understanding and Managing Organisational Change. Mabey, C. and Mayon-White, B (eds) Managing Change, 2nd Edition. London: Open University/Paul Chapman Publishing.

Watkins, J.M., Cooperrider,D.L.(2000). Appreciative Inquiry: A transformative paradigm. Journal of the Organization Development Network. Vol.32. 6-12.

Whitney,D. (1998). Let's Change the Subject and Change our Organization: an Appreciative Inquiry Approach to Organization Change.

More books by this author

How to Manage Teams: The No Waffle Guide to Managing Your Team Effectively

Presentation Skills: Portraying Confidence, Answering Tricky Questions and Structuring Content

How to Manage People: The No Waffle Guide to Managing Performance, Change and Stress in the Workplace

How to Manage Stress in the Workplace: The No Waffle Guide for Managers (EBook Only)

Manager's Guide to Providing Feedback: The No Waffle Guide to Providing Feedback and Rewards (EBook Only)

Coaching Skills for Managers: The No Waffle Guide to Getting the Best from Your Team (EBook Only)

What Other Marketing Books Won't Tell You: A Brutally Honest Account of Marketing a Small Business

The Counselling Sessions: Overcoming Feelings of Irritability and Anger in Relationships

The Counselling Sessions: Overcoming Anxiety and Panic Attacks

The Counselling Sessions: Overcoming Low Mood and Depression

20131995R00022

Printed in Poland
by Amazon Fulfillment
Poland Sp. z o.o., Wrocław